Lawful Permanent Residents

(GREEN CARD HOLDERS)

A Supplement to *First Steps: An LIRS Guide for Refugees, Asylum Seekers, and Migrants Released from Detention*

Edition 2014

2014 Lutheran Immigration & Refugee Service

Started by Lutheran congregations in 1939, Lutheran Immigration and Refugee Service (LIRS) is a national organization walking with migrants and refugees through ministries of service and justice, transforming U.S. communities by ensuring that newcomers are not only self-sufficient but also become connected and contributing members of their adopted communities in the United States.

Information in this manual may be reprinted with the following note: *Reprinted with permission of the Detained Torture Survivors' Legal Support Network, a program of Lutheran Immigration and Refugee Service.*

For information or bulk orders, contact:
firststeps@lirs.org

LIRS.org

Printed by LIRS Press
Printed in the U.S.A.

International Standard Book Number: 978-0-9908689-0-3

LAWFUL PERMANENT RESIDENTS

This resource provides specific information on rights, responsibilities, and benefits for lawful permanent residents (LPRs), also known as permanent resident aliens, legal permanent residents, and green card holders.

It is intended to supplement LIRS's publication titled, *First Steps: An LIRS Guide for Refugees, Asylum Seekers, and Migrants Released from Detention*. This document provides brief, status-specific information for LPRs. However, you should consult the *First Steps* guide, referenced here as "the Guide," for more detailed information and resources. It is available at www.lirs.org/firststeps.

For more detailed information on topics that appear in this publication, please refer to the following sections in the Guide:

- Section One for general information, tips, and resources for living in the U.S. as an immigrant, including what to do in an emergency and how to find important resources.
- Section Two for details on legal rights and responsibilities,

LAWFUL PERMANENT RESIDENTS

including information on legal services, the immigration consequences of criminal convictions, your rights when arrested or detained, and requirements for changing your address, among other topics.
- Section Three for information on basic services and needs, including details on benefits, healthcare, education, and housing.
- Section Four for information on integration and community support, including religious and cultural groups, emotional support, financial tips, and lists of helpful resources including legal services.

Important! This guide provides information about the law; however, you should always consult with a lawyer if you have legal questions. Do not rely on this guide instead of seeking the advice of a lawyer. This resource has information about how to find a lawyer.

What Does "Lawful Permanent Resident" Mean?

The term "lawful permanent resident," also known as "LPR," has the same meaning as "permanent resident alien," "legal permanent resident," and "green card holder." Green cards used to be printed on green paper, but no longer are. If you are an LPR, the U.S. government allows you to live permanently in the U.S. as long as you do not commit particular crimes or otherwise violate the terms of your status.

If you are an LPR, the U.S. government allows you to

- Live and work permanently in the U.S., as long as you meet the requirements of your status, including renewing your green card and not committing crimes
- Work anywhere in the U.S. (except for certain jobs that

LAWFUL PERMANENT RESIDENTS

require U.S. citizenship)
- Apply to become a U.S. citizen once you are eligible (usually after five years)
- Own property in the U.S.
- Travel in and out of the country (with some restrictions)
- Have protection under U.S. law

As an LPR, you are required to

- Obey all laws of the U.S.
- File income taxes and report all income to the federal and state government
- If you are a male between the ages of 18 and 25, register with the Selective Service
- Change your address online or provide it in writing to the Department of Homeland Security (DHS) within 10 days anytime you move
- Renew your green card when it is about to expire

Important! LPR status is not always "permanent." Thousands of immigrants with LPR status, including refugees and asylees, are removed (deported) each year because of criminal convictions. Unless you have obtained U.S. citizenship, you could be removed because of a criminal conviction.

Being an LPR is a necessary first step before becoming a citizen of the U.S. You may apply for U.S. citizenship after meeting certain conditions, usually for five years, as an LPR. Details are below.

How to Become a Lawful Permanent Resident

If you are reading this, you probably already have your green card,

LAWFUL PERMANENT RESIDENTS

so feel free to skip ahead to the next section. This section contains very basic information about how to become an LPR. However, if you do not have your green card and wish to see more detailed information to help you learn whether and how you may apply, please see Chapter 10, "How to Get Your Green Card," in the Guide.

Applying to become an LPR is called "adjustment of status," or "AOS." First, you must figure out whether you are eligible to adjust, and the eligibility criteria are very strict. The main pathways to apply for LPR status are through family sponsorship (certain family relationships to U.S. citizens or LPRs), employment sponsorship, humanitarian status (which includes refugees, asylees, and other protection-based statuses), or one of several other special categories. See Chapter 10 for more details on eligibility. See also www.uscis.gov/green-card/green-card-processes-and-procedures/green-card-eligibility.

The steps to becoming an LPR vary by status and which options are available to you. Regardless of status, everyone must fill out an I-485, Application to Register Permanent Residence or Adjust Status. You can request the most recent version of Form I-485 by calling USCIS at 1-800-870-3676 or you can get the form online at www.uscis.gov/i-485. If you can, get help from a BIA accredited representative or a lawyer.

How Do I Check the Status of My Green Card Application?

If you have an application pending for a green card but do not know the status, check the status of your case at https://egov.uscis.gov/cris/Dashboard/CaseStatus.do. You can also call the USCIS National Customer Service Center at 1-800-375-5283. You will likely be asked for your name, date of birth, A-number, and a receipt

LAWFUL PERMANENT RESIDENTS

number for your pending application. If you never received a receipt number, USCIS probably did not receive your application.

How Do I Renew or Replace My Green Card?

Most green cards are valid for 10 years. You should renew your green card if it is expired, or if it will expire within the next six months. You can start the renewal process six months before your card will expire.

You should apply to replace your green card if your card has been lost, stolen, or damaged. You should also renew your green card if your name or any other information on it has changed.

To renew or replace your green card, file Form I-90, Application to Replace Permanent Resident Card. Make sure to read the instructions first, at www.uscis.gov/sites/default/files/files/form/i-90instr.pdf. You can do one of the following:

- File the petition online at www.uscis.gov/e-filing-i-90, or
- Print out the paper form at www.uscis.gov/sites/default/files/files/form/i-90.pdf and mail it to USCIS.
   If using U.S. Postal Service (USPS), send to:
      USCIS
      P.O. Box 21262
      Phoenix, AZ 85036
   If using USPS Express Mail/Courier, send to:
      USCIS
      Attention: I-90
      1820 E. Skyharbor, Circle S, Floor 1
      Suite 100
      Phoenix, AZ 85034

LAWFUL PERMANENT RESIDENTS

Note: Although your green card lasts for 10 years and is renewable at that point, you may become eligible to apply to become a U.S. citizen ("naturalize") after having LPR status for five years. There are many advantages to applying for citizenship including access to more jobs, benefits, civil rights such as the ability to vote, and the ability to bring more family members more quickly, among others. In addition, while LPRs can still lose their status and be deported for certain crimes, U.S. citizens cannot be deported. Information on how to naturalize appears below.

Important! Note for Conditional Permanent Residents
Some people have "conditional permanent residence," a type of permanent residence that lasts initially for two years, and must be changed at the end of this period to become permanent. You might have conditional status if you were married for less than two years when you received your green card, or if you got your green card by being an investor.

This means that your LPR status only lasts for two years, and you must file to "remove the condition" within 90 days before the two-year period ends and your status expires, or you will lose your LPR status. When you apply to remove the conditional status, if your application is approved, you will gain regular LPR status.

To remove the conditional status if you received your status based on marriage, file Form I-751, Petition to Remove Conditions on Residence. You will find the form and instructions at www.uscis.gov/i-751.

To remove the conditional status if you received your status based on entrepreneurship, file Form I-829, Petition by Entrepreneur to Remove Conditions. You will find the form and instructions at www.uscis.gov/i-829.

LAWFUL PERMANENT RESIDENTS

Important! If you are a permanent resident who is 18 years or older, you must carry your green card with you at all times. You should make a photocopy of your green card and keep it in a safe place at home.

How Do I Make Sure I Keep My Lawful Permanent Resident Status?

Although your status is "permanent," the permanence depends upon your compliance with the law and conditions of your status.

Abandonment
The government may find that you abandoned your permanent resident status, and will cancel your status and take away your green card, if you do any of the following things:

- Move to another country (the government will likely assume you intend to live there permanently).
- Travel out of the U.S. and remain abroad for more than a year without getting a reentry permit or returning resident visa. (However, the government may determine that you have abandoned your status if you remain outside the U.S. for even less than a year, so it is recommended you speak to a lawyer before planning a trip of six months or longer or that you simply avoid long trips.)
- Remain outside the U.S. for more than two years after getting a reentry permit, without getting a returning resident visa. (Again, such lengthy trips are not recommended until you have citizenship.)
- Fail to file income tax returns, even while living outside the U.S.
- Declare yourself a "nonimmigrant" on your tax returns.

LAWFUL PERMANENT RESIDENTS

Criminal Activity

You may lose your status as a lawful permanent resident (your green card) if you commit certain crimes that make you removable. Many crimes make you removable from the U.S., so it is best to know and obey the law at all times. Even minor things such as failing to pay bus or metro fare can threaten your status. See the Guide, Chapter 4, "What Are the Immigration Consequences of Criminal Convictions?" for important information.

Important! If you have been arrested and accused or convicted of criminal activity, you will likely need an immigration lawyer **and** a criminal defense lawyer. Make sure your criminal lawyer knows your immigration status—otherwise he or she might advise you to take action that could harm your status. Ask your immigration lawyer to communicate with your criminal defense lawyer to make sure they both have all the information they need to help you.

For a list of free or low-cost immigration legal services providers in your state, please visit the following websites:
- AILA (American Immigration Lawyers Association) Immigration Lawyer Referral Service: www.ailalawyer.com, (202-216-2400)
- National Lawyers Guild, National Immigration Project: www.nationalimmigrationproject.org, (617-227-9727)
- Immigration Law Help: www.immigrationlawhelp.org (search by state)
- EOIR Free Legal Services Provider List: www.justice.gov/eoir/probono/states.htm (search by state)

For more details, please see the Guide, Chapter 3, "Legal Services and Immigration Court," to learn about how to find legal services. You can also view a list of legal organizations, listed by state, in Chapter 27, "Directory of Immigration Legal Services Providers."

LAWFUL PERMANENT RESIDENTS

What Are My Rights If I Am Arrested?

It is very important that you know what your rights are if you are arrested. Please read the Guide, Chapter 5, "What Are Your Rights If You Have Been Arrested?" A brief summary is below.

Right to Remain Silent

If the police, ICE, Federal Bureau of Investigation (FBI), or any law enforcement agent approaches you for a criminal matter, you have the right to remain silent. This means that you do not have to answer any questions until you talk to your lawyer. However, **you do *not* have the right to lie to police or immigration officials.** This is a crime, and could result in your deportation and inability to return to the U.S. If you do not want to answer any questions, it is very important that you do not lie, but instead state that you wish to speak to a lawyer before answering questions.

The Right to Be Free from "Unreasonable Searches and Seizures"

If the police stop you on the street, an officer can frisk you, which means pat your clothing to see if you are carrying anything illegal. If they stop you in your car, they can search without a warrant if they have a good reason to suspect illegal activity. Usually to search or enter your house, the police must show you a warrant. If they do not have one, you do not have to let them in. Even if they have a warrant and enter, you still have the right to remain silent.

What If ICE (Immigration and Customs Enforcement) Arrests Me?

ICE officials may ask to see your immigration papers. Show them your green card. If you do not, they may arrest you. Do not lie about your status, or present fake papers or papers that belong to someone else.

LAWFUL PERMANENT RESIDENTS

Do not sign anything, especially an "Order of Voluntary Departure" or anything admitting that you used false identification or travel documents, without talking to a lawyer first.

If ICE detains you, they may decide to begin removal (deportation) proceedings, activate an old removal order (if you have one against you), hold you in custody, or release you. ICE must make this decision within 48 hours of placing you in detention. If they have not, ask for a list of free lawyers.

How Do I Get My Belongings Back After I Am Released?
If you were detained in immigration detention, you may need to take several steps to get your belongings back. See Chapter 6, "How to Get Your Personal Property After You Are Released from Detention," in the Guide.

What Must I Do When I Change My Address?

All non-citizens, including LPRs, must notify USCIS when they move. You must notify USCIS within 10 days of changing your address. Otherwise, you could be arrested, charged a fine, forced to serve time in jail, and possibly deported. To notify USCIS of your change of address, fill out Form AR-11, Change of Address, which you can find at: www.uscis.gov/ar-11.

Note that if you have an open case in Immigration Court or the BIA, you must also notify the court system that you are moving. You must notify them within five days of your move. You can get the change of address form from the Immigration Court or online at www.justice.gov/eoir/eoirforms/eoir33/ICadr33.htm if your case is in Immigration Court, and www.justice.gov/eoir/eoirforms/eoir33bia.pdf if your case is at the BIA.

LAWFUL PERMANENT RESIDENTS

For more information, see Chapter 8, "What You Must Do When You Change Your Address," in the Guide.

Can I Reunite with My Family?

As an LPR, you can apply to bring your spouse (husband or wife) or unmarried children of any age to the U.S.

You can begin by filing an I-130, Petition for an Alien Relative, which you can find at www.uscis.gov/i-130. You must include evidence that proves your LPR status (such as a copy of your green card), and evidence that proves your relationship, such as a birth or marriage certificate. You must also include a filing fee of $420. For detailed instructions on how and where to apply, as well as other evidence you may need to include, see USCIS's instructions at www.uscis.gov/sites/default/files/files/form/i-130instr.pdf.

Once USCIS approves your I-130, your application is sent to the National Visa Center, which places your relatives in a line of people from the same country who are also the same type of relative (husband, wife, or child) from that country. This line can be very long and take years to go through, so it is best to apply as soon as you can. You may view the "Visa Bulletins" section on the State Department website to see current approximate wait times: http://travel.state.gov/content/visas/english.html. Once your relative reaches the front of the line, the National Visa Center will begin processing the case, and will instruct you to submit fees and a number of new forms, including a passport; photographs; civil documents (such as marriage and birth certificates); medical forms; Form DS-260, Immigrant Visa and Alien Registration Application (which you will submit online at the time); and Form I-864, Affidavit of Support, which asks for financial information to prove you have

LAWFUL PERMANENT RESIDENTS

the ability to support your relative upon arrival. You can find it here: www.uscis.gov/i-864.

Once the National Visa Center has approved your application, they will schedule an interview for your relative with the U.S. State Department. This is the final step in the process. You may read more about the process here: http://travel.state.gov/content/visas/english/immigrate/types/family/family-preference.html.

If you have filed for a spouse, when your spouse reaches the top of the list, his or her unmarried children under 21 can usually follow to join on your spouse's visa. However, if your spouse's child turns 21 before your spouse reaches the top of the list, you will need to file a new separate petition for each child included on the original petition.

If you have applied for your unmarried child, if that child marries, his or her petition will be immediately taken away, because LPRs cannot bring married children.

However, if you become a U.S. citizen before your child marries, you can continue by filing a new I-130 for your child. U.S. citizens can bring more family members, including married children of any age, parents, and siblings, although they have different wait times. Details are in the following section on becoming a U.S. citizen.

You should get help from a BIA accredited organization or lawyer to help you file this form. Carefully read the instructions, and keep these things in mind:

- You will need proof that the people you want to bring are your relatives. Photographs, birth certificates, and marriage certificates will help you prove this.

LAWFUL PERMANENT RESIDENTS

- You will have to pay for the airplane tickets for your family members.
- Make sure you include copies of all necessary supporting documents mentioned in the Form I-130 instructions. USCIS may delay or deny your application if these supporting documents are not included.
- After you file your immigration form, USCIS may write a letter telling you that your relative will need to have a biometrics appointment. They may also ask for a signature and take a picture. Sometimes, a DNA test may be required for you and for the relative you are applying to bring. You may have to pay for these tests.
- Keep a photocopy of the completed form for your records. Send the form via certified mail with a return receipt, available at the post office.

How Do I Become a Citizen?

What is Naturalization?
Naturalization is the process by which certain non-U.S. citizens can apply to become U.S. citizens. To "naturalize" means to take the required steps to become a U.S. citizen.

What Are the Benefits of Naturalizing?
When you naturalize, you will become a U.S. citizen, and have almost all the same rights and protections as U.S. born citizens. U.S. citizens have more rights than lawful permanent residents (LPRs). There are many things only U.S. citizens can do in America, some of which may be very important to you. It is very important for you try to naturalize when you are eligible, so you may receive these rights and protections. As a naturalized U.S. citizen, you will be able to:

LAWFUL PERMANENT RESIDENTS

- **Keep your lawful status in the United States and no longer be in danger of deportation.**
  This is very important! Even if you have adjusted your status to become an LPR (have your green card) you can still have your green card taken away and be deported for committing certain crimes, traveling outside the U.S. for too long, or failing to file your income taxes. When you are an American citizen, you cannot be deported.
- **Bring family members to the U.S.**
  U.S. citizens can bring more family members to the U.S. than refugee, asylees, and LPRs. For example, as a refugee or asylee, you can apply for your spouse (husband or wife) and any unmarried children under the age of 21 to join you. As an LPR, you may apply to bring your spouse or unmarried children of any age. But as a U.S. citizen, you may apply to bring your spouse, and children of any age, whether they are unmarried or married. And as a U.S. citizen, you may also apply to bring your parents and siblings (brother and sisters) once you are over 21 years old.
- **Get more government benefits.**
  Immigrants have many restrictions on access to government benefits and healthcare. (See Chapters 18 and 19 for details on immigrants' access to benefits and healthcare.) However, after you naturalize, you will no longer be subject to immigration-related restrictions, and will have access to benefits and healthcare according to the same rules as U.S. citizens.
- **Vote.**
  Only U.S. citizens can vote in federal elections. Many states also only allow U.S. citizens to vote in state elections. Voting to elect officials like the President and members of Congress is an important political right to many U.S. citizens.

LAWFUL PERMANENT RESIDENTS

- **Serve on a jury.**
  Only U.S. citizens can serve on a federal jury, and many states also only allow U.S. citizens to serve on a jury. Juries help judges make decisions in court cases.
- **Travel abroad with a U.S. passport.**
  You will be able to travel abroad without restrictions on how long you can stay outside the U.S. You will also be able to get help from the U.S. government when you are abroad if you need it.
- **Get U.S. citizenship for children under 18 years of age.**
  Generally, a child born abroad to a U.S. citizen automatically becomes a U.S. citizen. Any children you previously had who were born abroad and were under 18 at the time you become a citizen may also be eligible to become a U.S. citizen. See a lawyer for help with either of these situations. (Children born inside the U.S. are automatically U.S. citizens.)
- **Apply for more federal jobs.**
  Some federal jobs require U.S. citizenship.
- **Become an elected government official.**
  Only U.S. citizens can run in federal elections for the U.S. Senate or House of Representatives, and most state and local governments have similar rules for state and local government positions. Unfortunately, only those born in the U.S. can run for President.
- **Become eligible for more federal grants and scholarships.**
  Many financial aid grants, including college scholarships, are available only to U.S. citizens.

Note: Before you decide to apply to naturalize, you should first determine if you might already be a U.S. citizen. If you were born in the U.S. or a U.S. territory, or if at least one of your parents is a U.S. citizen, you may already be a U.S. citizen. If either of these

LAWFUL PERMANENT RESIDENTS

situations apply to you, see an immigration lawyer immediately to find out whether you may already be a citizen.

Am I Eligible to Become a U.S. Citizen?
You must meet **all** of the following criteria to apply for naturalization:

- Be at least 18 years old, AND
- Have been admitted as lawful permanent resident (LPR) for at least five years (with some exceptions, explained below), AND
- Have "continuous residence" (explained below) in the U.S. for at least five years after receiving your LPR status (green card), AND
- Have been physically present in the U.S. for at least 30 months of the five-year period before applying for naturalization, AND
- Have lived in the state in which you plan to apply for at least three months before applying, AND
- Live in the U.S. continuously from the time of application for naturalization to the time of admission as a U.S. citizen, AND
- Have good moral character (explained below), AND
- Can demonstrate knowledge of civics and English, and pledge allegiance to the Constitution.

Five Years of Lawful Permanent Residence
Typically, naturalization requires five years of status as a green card, or lawful permanent resident. There are however some exceptions:

- Refugees and asylees who adjusted their status and got their green card (LPR status) after one year may count that one year as part of the five. In other words, refugees and asylees may apply to naturalize after having a green card for four years, instead of five.

LAWFUL PERMANENT RESIDENTS

- If you are applying to naturalize based on your marriage to a U.S. citizen, you may apply after having your green card for three years, instead of five.
- If you have qualifying experience as a U.S. military member, you may be eligible to apply earlier. For more information, see USCIS's page on Citizenship for Military Members at www.uscis.gov/military/citizenship-military-personnel-family-members/citizenship-military-members and talk to a lawyer.

Continuous Residence
"Continuous residence" means that you have lived in the U.S., and maintained the U.S. as your place of residence (and no other country) on a continuous basis for five years. You can travel and still maintain continuous residence, but there are important restrictions:

- Traveling outside the U.S. and staying outside for a period of six to twelve months in a row may interrupt this period of "continuous residence," meaning you may have to start over.
- Traveling outside the U.S. for a continuous period of one year or longer will most likely interrupt your period of "continuous residence," and you will have to start over.

It is highly recommended that if you travel outside the U.S., you stay abroad for less than six months; otherwise you could lose your period of continuous residence and have to start your five-year waiting period over. There are a few exceptions if you stayed out between six months and one year, but you should see a lawyer for help if that is the case.

"Continuous residence" also means you must file and pay your taxes every year as a lawful permanent resident (LPR). You may not claim "nonresident alien status" on your tax forms to avoid paying

LAWFUL PERMANENT RESIDENTS

your taxes, or you will lose your continuous residence.

<u>Good Moral Character</u>
To become a U.S. citizen, you must demonstrate that you have "good moral character." Generally, this means someone who is honest, pays their taxes, does not commit crimes, and pays their debts.

If you have committed certain crimes, you will never be able to establish good moral character, and will never be able to apply for citizenship. These crimes include murder and any "aggravated felony" of which you were convicted after November 29, 1990. Other crimes may temporarily prevent you from proving you have good moral character and applying for citizenship, but after a period of time, you will be able to apply. If you have been arrested or convicted of any crimes, and wish to naturalize, it is important to see a lawyer to help you determine whether your crimes will permanently or temporarily prevent you from showing good moral character and naturalizing.

Some examples of crimes that might prevent you from showing good moral character include any crime committed with intent to harm someone, using or selling drugs, being married to more than one person at a time, failing to pay court-ordered child support or alimony payments, and lying to gain immigration benefits, among others.

How Do I Become a U.S. Citizen?
To apply for U.S. citizenship, you must first determine whether you are eligible according to the above criteria. You also can work through USCIS's Naturalization Worksheet, available at www.uscis.gov/sites/default/files/USCIS/Resources/Citizenship%20%26%20Naturalization%20Based%20Resources/A%20Guide%20to%20

LAWFUL PERMANENT RESIDENTS

Naturalization/PDFs/M-480.pdf. This worksheet outlines the rules above and helps you determine if you are eligible.

File Form N-400, Application for Naturalization
If you are eligible, you must file Form N-400, Application for Naturalization. Visit USCIS's page on the N-400 at www.uscis.gov/n-400. Before you fill out the N-400, you should

- Read USCIS's Guide to Naturalization (www.uscis.gov/sites/default/files/files/article/M-476.pdf), or get your lawyer or someone at a BIA accredited organization to help you read through and understand it, because the N-400 application makes many references to this document.
- Then, read the N-400 Instructions, available at www.uscis.gov/sites/default/files/files/form/n-400instr.pdf.

Download the N-400, Application for Naturalization at www.uscis.gov/sites/default/files/files/form/n-400.pdf.

Fill out your N-400 carefully, in blue or black ink. It is highly recommended that you get a lawyer or BIA accredited representative to help you. Be sure to put your A-number at the top right-hand corner of each page. Check your information for accuracy, and sign it. Before you file, make sure you have all the required documentation!

Note: Your N-400 asks questions about crimes. It is very important that you answer honestly and report all crimes, even ones you may have gotten expunged (removed) from your record. If you do not tell USCIS about these crimes, they will find out, and may deny your application, even if the crime you failed to report was not a crime that would have caused your application to be denied!

LAWFUL PERMANENT RESIDENTS

<u>What Do I Include with My Application?</u>
You must submit the following with your application:

- Two identical 2x2 passport-style photos taken within 30 days of filing. Write your name and A-number lightly on the back.
- A copy of your green card.
- The filing fee ($595) and the fee for your biometrics (fingerprinting) appointment ($85).
- Form N-648, Medical Certification for Disability Exceptions **only if you are seeking a medical or age-related exception to the English or civics test requirements** (see below). You may find Form N-648 at www.uscis.gov/n-648.

<u>Where Do I Mail My Application?</u>
Where you should mail your application depends on where you live, so check USCIS's instructions at www.uscis.gov/n-400. Be sure to make copies and ask for a certified mail receipt!

<u>When Can I File My Application?</u>
You may generally file your application up to 90 days before you've had continuous residence as an LPR for five years (or for a refugee, four years) and met the other specific requirements outlined above.

<u>What Must I Do After I File My Application?</u>
There are still several steps you must take after you submit your application.

Biometrics Appointment
After USCIS receives your application, USCIS will contact you to let you know when you should go to your local USCIS Application Support Center (ASC) for your biometrics (fingerprinting) appointment. USCIS will take your fingerprints and conduct a criminal background check.

LAWFUL PERMANENT RESIDENTS

Naturalization Interview
USCIS will schedule an interview for you. Be sure to attend this interview on time, and let USCIS know immediately if you have to reschedule. You must bring the following to your naturalization interview:

- A copy of your green card (LPR card).
- A valid state ID (a form of identification, such as a driver's license, issued by your state).
- Your passport and any travel documents.
- Other relevant documents. Depending on your situation, you may have other documents you should bring. For example, if you were arrested or convicted of a crime, you must bring arrest or court documents. If you had to serve probation, you should bring proof that you completed your probation. For more information on other documents you may want to bring, see USCIS's Guide to Naturalization, at www.uscis.gov/sites/default/files/files/article/M-476.pdf.

Several things will happen at your Naturalization Interview.

1. **Interview:** USCIS will ask you questions about what you wrote on your N-400. You should bring a copy so you can look at it.
2. **Civics and English Tests:** You will take two tests, an English test and a civics test. You should dedicate a lot of time to studying before the interview. You can access study materials for both tests at www.uscis.gov/citizenship/learners/study-test. Many local community groups that help immigrants offer classes to help you prepare. You can find classes and resources at www.uscis.gov/citizenship/learners/find-help-your-community. If you fail, you will be able to retake it only once. If you fail twice, your application will be denied.

LAWFUL PERMANENT RESIDENTS

    a. The English test will consist of three parts that assess your speaking ability, reading ability, and writing ability. You can access information on the test, study materials, and practice tests at www.uscis.gov/citizenship/learners/study-test/study-materials-english-test.

    b. The civics test will test your knowledge of American history and government. There are 100 questions on the civics test, and the USCIS officer will pick 10 to ask you. You must get 6 questions correct to pass. You may find the questions by visiting: www.uscis.gov/citizenship/learners/study-test and clicking on the link for "100 civics questions on the naturalization test." But remember the answers to certain questions about elected officials may change with elections, so make sure you have the most up-to-date information. You can access information on the test, study materials, and practice tests at www.uscis.gov/citizenship/learners/study-test/study-materials-civics-test.

Exceptions to the Test Requirements: You may not have to take the English test if you are over 50 years old and have lived in the U.S. as an LPR for over 20 years, or if you are over 55 years old and have lived in the U.S. for over 15 years. You may not have to take the civics test if you have certain physical or mental disabilities. For more details, see www.uscis.gov/us-citizenship/citizenship-through-naturalization/exceptions-accommodations. If you are seeking such an exception, you must submit a Form N-648, Medical Certification for Disability Exceptions, with your N-400, Application for Naturalization. You may find it at www.uscis.gov/n-648.

USCIS will usually provide you with a notice of your results the same

LAWFUL PERMANENT RESIDENTS

day. However, sometimes the USCIS officer will not be able to make a decision, and may need to continue your case. The officer may then require a second interview, or ask for additional evidence. If USCIS does not need further information, the officer will either approve your application if you provide evidence that establishes your eligibility, or deny it if your interview, test results, and evidence do not show you are eligible to naturalize.

What Can I Do if USCIS Denies My Application?
If your application was denied, USCIS will provide a written explanation with the reasons for denial. If you think USCIS incorrectly denied your application, you may request a hearing to appeal. You must file Form N-336, Request for a Hearing on a Decision in Naturalization Proceedings, available at www.uscis.gov/n-336. **You must file this appeal, with the filing fee, within 30 days of your denial, or the decision will be final.**

What Happens After USCIS Approves My Application?
USCIS will mail you a notice to take the Oath of Allegiance, with the date, time, and location of your oath ceremony. Occasionally, you may be able to take the Oath of Allegiance the same day your application is approved after your interview. If you cannot attend your ceremony, return the notice and explain why you cannot attend, and request a rescheduled ceremony.

During your ceremony, you will take an Oath of Allegiance to the U.S. Remember to bring your green card, because you will turn it in after the ceremony, and receive a Certificate of Naturalization, which certifies that you are a naturalized American citizen. Congratulations!

Important! You must still notify USCIS if you change your address

LAWFUL PERMANENT RESIDENTS

after you submit your N-400 application and while you are waiting to complete the process and become a citizen. You must call Customer Service at 1-800-375-5283 (TTY: 1-800-767-1833), and fill out an AR-11, Alien's Change of Address Card, and submit it to USCIS within 10 days of your move. See the Guide's Chapter 8, "What You Must Do When You Change Your Address," for more details.

How Do I Prove My Status When I Get Citizenship?
You will receive a Form N-550, Certificate of Naturalization, after you take your Oath of Allegiance to the U.S. This proves your status as an American citizen. If you lose this certificate, you must submit Form N-565, Application for Replacement Naturalization/Citizenship Document, available at www.uscis.gov/n-565.

What Should I Do When I Naturalize?
Update Your Social Security Record
After you naturalize, you must update your Social Security record. It is important for Social Security to have updated records on your citizenship. This will make it easier for you to access the benefits and rights to which you are entitled as a U.S. citizen, including Social Security and other government benefits. Wait at least 10 days after your naturalization ceremony, then call Social Security at 1-800-772-1213 or visit www.socialsecurity.gov to make an appointment. Remember to bring your Certificate of Naturalization or U.S. Passport.

Register to Vote
You may now register to vote if you wish to vote in elections. You may do this in person, by mail, at public assistance offices, or when you apply to renew your driver's license. Visit the U.S. Election Assistance Commission at www.eac.gov.

LAWFUL PERMANENT RESIDENTS

Apply for a U.S. Passport if You Wish to Travel Abroad
After you naturalize, you are also eligible to apply for a U.S. passport, which will allow you to travel abroad as a U.S. citizen and receive help from U.S. embassies or consulates abroad if you need it. Visit www.travel.state.gov to download the application forms and find the passport acceptance facility near you.

Apply for Your LPR Children Under 18
If you have any children who were born abroad, are lawful permanent residents, and are under 18 on the day you naturalized, they may have automatically become U.S. citizens as well, and you may want to apply for proof of their status. You may apply for a U.S. passport for your child, or apply for a Certificate of Citizenship using Form N-600, Application for Certificate of Citizenship, available at www.uscis.gov/n-600k.

Apply to Sponsor Relatives Abroad to Come to the U.S.
You may now also apply to sponsor additional relatives to come to the U.S. You will be applying for these family members to get a green card. As a U.S. citizen, you may apply to bring your immediate relatives. The "immediate relative" category includes your husband or wife, unmarried children under the age of 21, and parents (as long as you are over 21). These applications are processed immediately and there is no waitlist.

You may also apply to bring other family members who fit into a "family preference category." This category includes your unmarried sons or daughters over the age of 21, married children of any age, and your brothers and sisters (as long as you are over 21). The government has a limited number of visas available for these family members each year, and they go on a waitlist for family members in each category. The waitlist can be quite long and it can take years.

LAWFUL PERMANENT RESIDENTS

For more information on how to bring your family members who are still abroad to the U.S., please see USCIS's website on sponsoring family members at www.uscis.gov/green-card/green-card-through-family, and see an immigration lawyer for help.

Can I Travel Outside of the United States?

As a lawful permanent resident, you can travel within and outside of the U.S. with a valid green card, but with some restrictions. It is important that you know the risks of traveling outside of the U.S. if you are not a U.S. citizen.

If you want to travel outside of the U.S., you will need a passport from the country where you are a citizen and may need a travel visa from your destination country. To re-enter the U.S., you will need a valid, unexpired green card, and other qualifying identification documents such as a passport, foreign national identification (ID) card, or U.S. driver's license.

Permanent residents who leave the U.S. for extended periods, or who cannot show their intent to live permanently in the U.S., may lose their permanent resident status because USCIS may decide you have abandoned your status. In general, leaving the U.S. for less than one year is not seen as abandoning your right to permanent residency status. To determine if you have abandoned your status, an officer will evaluate your connection to the U.S. by looking at your family and community ties, mailing address, bank accounts, driver's license, and property. Many immigrants believe they can live abroad as long as they return to the U.S. at least once a year. This is incorrect.

If you think you will be out of the U.S. for more than one year, you

LAWFUL PERMANENT RESIDENTS

should apply for a re-entry permit before leaving the country. Having a re-entry permit does not guarantee that you will be admitted to the U.S. when you return, but it can make it easier to show that you are returning from a temporary visit abroad. File Form I-131, Application for Travel Document, 60 days prior to your departure date to establish your intent to return and permanently reside in the U.S. You can request the most recent version of Form I-131 by calling USCIS at 1-800-870-3676 or you can get the form online at www.uscis.gov/i-131. There is a fee to file Form I-131. A re-entry permit is valid for up to two years. You will show the re-entry permit at a port of entry.

If you plan to naturalize, or become a U.S. citizen, you should not travel outside the U.S. for more than six months at a time. Staying outside the U.S. for longer than six months can keep you from meeting the "continuous residence" requirement for naturalization. If you plan to naturalize and must travel outside the U.S. for a year or longer for very limited reasons such as necessity for certain jobs, you may file Form N-470, Application to Preserve Residence for Naturalization Purposes, available at www.uscis.gov/n-470. Be sure to read the instructions carefully to learn whether you are eligible and whether the N-470 will preserve your period of continuous residence so you can still naturalize. Ask for help if you are unsure.

Important! If you have committed a crime, you will likely not be able to re-enter the U.S. if you leave. Even if your crime did not make you "deportable," it could make you "inadmissible," which means Immigration will not let you enter the U.S.

Can I Vote?

As an LPR, you are not allowed to vote in federal elections. Although

LAWFUL PERMANENT RESIDENTS

a few states and local governments allow you to vote in state and local elections, it is very uncommon. Failure to abide by the above requirements can jeopardize your immigration status and make you subject to deportation.

What Is the Selective Service, and Am I Required to Sign Up?

All men between ages 18 and 25 living in the U.S., regardless of immigration status, must register for Selective Service. Registering tells the government that you are available to serve in the U.S. Armed Forces if the government ever orders a military draft. However, the U.S. government has not had a draft since the 1970's, and it is highly unlikely that there will ever be a draft again. This means permanent residents and citizens do not have to serve in the Armed Forces unless they want to. The Selective Service is just a required backup for emergencies.

If you have a Social Security number, you can go online to register for Selective Service at https://www.sss.gov/RegVer/wfRegistration.aspx. Or you can go to any post office and fill out the Selective Service form. Bring your Social Security card. If you do not have a Social Security number, you will have to send a copy of your Social Security card when you get one. When you send it, also put your complete name, date of birth, Selective Service registration number, and current mailing address. You can send it to:

Selective Service System
P.O. Box 94636
Palatine, IL 60094-4636

To speak with someone from the Selective Service, call 847-688-6888.

LAWFUL PERMANENT RESIDENTS

Can I Join the Military?

As an LPR, you can apply to join the military, but you will not be able to receive top-security clearance positions until you are a U.S. citizen. If you are interested in joining the military, you should speak to a recruiter or see www.military.com/join-armed-forces.

Do I Have the Right to Work?

A green card allows you to work in the U.S. without restrictions on location or type of employment. When applying for a job, a green card establishes your identity and proves that you are authorized to work in the U.S. Receiving LPR status means that you are authorized to work and that you do not have to apply with USCIS for a work permit.

Note: There are some jobs that are reserved for U.S. citizens, usually jobs with the government that require high-level security clearances.

How Do I Show Employers that I Am Eligible to Work?
You must show your employer two documents to work—a photo document that proves your identity and a document that proves you have the legal right to work. USCIS Form I-9, found at www.uscis.gov/sites/default/files/files/form/i-9.pdf, has a list of what documents you can show your employer. If you have a green card, you only need to show that, because it has your photograph and shows that you have the right to work.

If you can, it is best to show your employer that you meet the I-9 requirements without using an immigration document such as a green card. For example, use your Social Security card and driver's license. Otherwise, your employer may incorrectly think your work

LAWFUL PERMANENT RESIDENTS

authorization is limited. If you can satisfy the I-9 requirements with other documents listed on the I-9 form, the employer is not allowed to require you to show your green card.

Confusion About Employment Authorization

Sometimes employers get confused about your right to work or the documents you need to show. Sometimes they want to see a green card or a work permit, even though you have shown them all the required documents. Some employers may use a system on the Internet called E-Verify to check your right to work. They can find E-Verify at www.dhs.gov/e-verify. You can enter your information on E-Verify to find out what an employer will see if they check online at www.uscis.gov/everifyselfcheck. You can go online to http://www.nilc.org/materialsev.html to find a "Know Your Rights About E-Verify" document, available in English and Spanish.

If you or your employer have questions about what documents are needed, you can call the Office of Special Counsel for Immigration-Related Unfair Employment Practices in the Department of Justice. You should call the Worker Information Hotline at 800-255-7688, or your employer can call the Employer Information Hotline at 800-255-8155. See www.usdoj.gov/crt/osc for further information. For more on the right and authorization to work, see Chapter 14, "The Right to Work," and Chapter 15, "How to Get a Work Permit," in the Guide.

Can I Get a Social Security Number (SSN)?

As an LPR, you are eligible for a Social Security number (SSN). An SSN is a 9-digit number the U.S. government assigns to U.S. citizens, lawful permanent residents, and other lawfully present individuals. The government uses it to track your income from working to determine how much tax you owe, as you must pay tax if you work.

LAWFUL PERMANENT RESIDENTS

The government will also use your SSN to determine how much to give you in Social Security benefits when you reach full retirement age or become disabled and no longer have income.

You also need an SSN to access certain benefits and rights you may be entitled to. Local offices of social services agencies will use your SSN to see what benefits you qualify for. Employers, banks, and departments of motor vehicles may ask for your SSN. If you apply for federal financial aid to study for college, the college or university will ask for your SSN. For these reasons, it is best to get one as soon as you can.

Your SSN is unique to you, and you should be very careful to keep your Social Security card safe and to not let other people know your SSN, because this could put you at risk for identity theft. Identity theft is when someone steals your personal information and uses it without your permission.

How Do I Get a Social Security Number?
You should apply for and receive a Social Security card, a physical card that contains your SSN. You will have to visit a Social Security Administration (SSA) office in person to complete and sign Form SS-5, Application for a Social Security Card. You may review and print this form online at www.ssa.gov/online/ss-5.pdf. For more information, call 1-800-772-1213. For the deaf or hearing-impaired, call the TTY number 1-800-325-0778.

Find your local SSA office at www.socialsecurity.gov/locator. You must bring original documents or copies certified by the issuing agency showing 1) work-authorized immigration status, 2) age, and 3) identity.

LAWFUL PERMANENT RESIDENTS

1. You can show several types of documents to prove your work-authorized immigration status, such as your green card or I-94. For a list of documents you can use to prove your status, view Social Security's list at www.ssa.gov/pubs/EN-05-10096.pdf, and see the Guide's Chapter 7, "Case Status and Proof of Status."
2. To show your age, you may submit your birth certificate, U.S. hospital record of your birth, passport, or green card.
3. To prove your identity, you must submit a document that is current, and that shows your name, identifying information, and preferably a photograph. If you don't have the documents the SSA requests, they may ask to see one of the following: employee ID card, school ID card, health insurance card (not including Medicare), U.S. military ID card, adoption decree, life insurance policy, or a marriage document in the event of a name change.

The SSA office may use a single document to show more than one thing (for example, your green card proves both your work authorization and your age). You will need to bring at least two documents to the SSA office to qualify to receive a Social Security card. After you have submitted your form, ask for a receipt, which is the proof that you applied.

There is no charge for an SSN or card. If anyone tries to charge you, you can report them by calling 800-269-0271.

What If I Do Not Receive My Social Security Card?
You should receive your Social Security card in the mail within 10 days. If you do not, you can either return to your local office to ask, or call 1-800-772-1213. Take the documents you originally presented as evidence, or have them available if you call.

LAWFUL PERMANENT RESIDENTS

If you have already applied for an SSN but your employer needs to verify your name and SSN immediately, they can use the online SSN Verification Service at www.ssa.gov/employer/ssnv.htm or call the Telephone Number Employer Verification, which is explained at www.ssa.gov/employer/documents/TNEV.pdf.

Can I Get a State Identification (ID) Card?

As an LPR, you are eligible to get a state ID card. In the U.S., most standard ID cards are issued by the state in which you live. The card will usually show your photograph, signature, address, date of birth, sex, eye color, hair color, height, and weight. A state ID card is a helpful document. You can show it to employers, landlords, banks, and other businesses to prove who you are. Many immigrants find it helpful to get a state ID card, even though it can be difficult, because unlike your I-94 or green card, your state ID card does not mention your immigration status or how long you have been in the U.S.

Many Americans over the age of 16 choose to get a driver's license so they can legally drive. Driver's licenses are also issued by the state in which you live. Most people use their driver's license as state ID, so if you get a license, you do not need to get a separate state ID. Information on obtaining a driver's license appears below.

How Do I Get an ID?
It will cost money to get a state ID. Each state has different rules about getting an ID card. Call your local Department of Motor Vehicles (DMV) office to find out what documents you will need to obtain a state ID card. You can locate the nearest DMV office in the phone book or on the Internet. The DMV may have a different name in your state. It may be called the "motor vehicle administration" (MVA) or the "division of motor vehicles" or something else.

LAWFUL PERMANENT RESIDENTS

Depending on your state, you may also be allowed to get a driver's license. This will be expensive and will involve taking driving classes and passing a driving test. **You cannot drive in the U.S. unless you have a driver's license. If you do drive without a license, you could be arrested. You also cannot drink alcohol and drive, because it is dangerous. Driving without a license and driving while under the influence of alcohol can both lead to your deportation.** Because it takes a long time to learn to drive and obtain your license, you may want to get a state ID first, and worry about driving later.

Important! The paperwork to get your driver's license or other state ID card is long and confusing. There are many questions that ask you to "check" (√) or mark boxes that ask confusing questions. One asks if you would like to vote. **Do not check this box.** If you do, you will become registered to vote, which is illegal for noncitizens. If you register to vote before you are a citizen, you may not be allowed to become a citizen! It is best to take someone such as your lawyer or a friend who is fluent in English to help you.

What if I Have Problems Getting My State ID Card?
People who work at the DMV may not understand your immigration status, or what documents are required for your status. Ask them to write down which documents you need. If they decline your application, ask them to write down why your documents do not meet the requirements. Ask them to write down their name and office phone number. Getting an ID can be difficult even for U.S. citizens. Try to be patient. If they still do not understand, ask someone at an immigrant's rights community or advocacy group, or your lawyer, to explain it to them.

LAWFUL PERMANENT RESIDENTS

What Public Benefits Can I Access?

You may be eligible for some forms of government-funded assistance if you do not make enough money to pay for food, medical care, and other basic life needs. The rules on eligibility for public benefits are very complex. Please see the Guide's Chapter 18, "How to Get Public Benefits and Financial Support," for more detailed information. Additionally, the National Immigration Law Center (NILC) offers expertise in the area of benefits for immigrants. Visit http://nilc.org/access-to-bens.html for information on access and eligibility for various types of benefits.

Access to Federal "Means-Tested Benefits"

As an LPR, you are considered a "qualified" immigrant, which means you qualify for some government benefits, subject to restrictions. However, many qualified immigrants, including LPRs, are excluded from a lot of benefits at first. There are five types of benefits, known as "means-tested benefits," that impose a five-year or longer waiting period for many qualified immigrants:

- Medicaid (except for emergency Medicaid, which is always available)
- CHIP (Children's Health Insurance Program)
- TANF (Temporary Assistance for Needy Families)—but your state will probably have a different name for it
- SNAP (Supplemental Nutrition Assistance Program, or food stamps) for adults
- SSI (Supplemental Security Income)

The federal government runs SSI and SNAP (even though you must apply through your state agency) using a standard set of eligibility

LAWFUL PERMANENT RESIDENTS

rules throughout the country. This means the rules about who is eligible for SSI and SNAP are the same in each state.

However, TANF, Medicaid, and CHIP are administered differently by each state, and each state may implement different rules on eligibility. This means even if you are qualified and subject to the 5-year federal bar according to federal law, you might be eligible for some of these programs immediately in your state. **It is important to read about each program, and especially check with your state if the benefit you seek is either a state-funded benefit or a federally-funded state-administered benefit.**

Federal Public Benefits Available to All Qualified Immigrants
Some other types of benefits, simply known as "federal public benefits," are available to all qualified immigrants (including LPRs), with no restrictions and no 5-year bar. These benefits include loans, contracts, grants, and licenses provided or funded by a U.S. government agency. They also include other benefits such as retirement, unemployment, some health, disability, welfare, post-secondary education, assisted housing, public housing, and food assistance provided by a U.S. government agency. Ask your state social services agency for details.

Basic Emergency Benefits Available to All Immigrants, Regardless of Status
All immigrants are always eligible for the following, regardless of status: Emergency Medicaid, immunizations/treatment of communicable diseases, school breakfasts and lunches, WIC (food assistance program for women, infants, and children), and short-term noncash emergency disaster assistance. The following other in-kind services necessary to protect life and safety (as long as no income qualifications are required for eligibility) are also available

LAWFUL PERMANENT RESIDENTS

to everyone: child/adult protective services; federal programs that address weather emergencies and homelessness; shelters for domestic violence victims, runaway children, and the homeless; soup kitchens; community food banks; Meals-On-Wheels; medical, public health, and mental health services necessary to protect public safety; violence and abuse prevention; disability and substance abuse services necessary to protect life and safety; and programs that protect safety of children, workers, and community residents. Additionally, if federal funds are provided to a state as a block grant to a hospital, shelter, or other services agency, they are not considered federal public benefits, and should be available to everyone, regardless of status.

Important! Accepting cash public assistance payments (like SSI and TANF) can create problems with USCIS that could prevent you from staying in the U.S. permanently or naturalizing. The government may worry you will become a "public charge," which means someone permanently dependent on the government to survive. This applies to LPRs and could jeopardize your chances of naturalizing. Check with a lawyer or BIA-recognized organization about your eligibility.

As you can see, it is hard for many immigrants, even those with green cards or other lawful statuses, to get benefits. Remember that once you become a U.S. citizen, you become eligible for all of the same benefits as American citizens, and restrictions or wait times based on immigration status no longer apply.

Note on Where to Apply and Interpretation
You can apply for most of these benefits at the Department of Social Services (a government agency) in your city or town. All agencies that are part of social services departments are required by law to provide you with an interpreter if you request one.

LAWFUL PERMANENT RESIDENTS

PUBLIC BENEFITS PROGRAMS

Can I Apply for the Matching Grant Program?
No, as an LPR, you are not eligible for benefits under the Matching Grant Program.

Can I Apply for Refugee Cash Assistance (RCA)?
No, as an LPR, you are not eligible for Refugee Cash Assistance (RCA) benefits.

Can I Apply for Supplemental Security Income (SSI)?
SSI is a U.S. government program that provides monthly stipends to low-income people who are blind, disabled, or age 65 or older. If you are not blind, disabled, or 65 or older, you cannot receive SSI.

Under very strict circumstances, you may be eligible to receive SSI benefits. LPRs are eligible to receive SSI if they meet the other program requirements:

- Were lawfully residing in the U.S. on August 22, 1996 and now have a disability, or
- Were receiving SSI on August 22, 1996, or
- Have credit for "40 qualifying quarters of work"* in the U.S., and have had LPR status for at least five years.

*A "qualifying quarter of work" is a three-month period in which enough income is earned to qualify as a "Social Security quarter." The Social Security Administration determines this amount each year. The shortest amount of time in which one person could earn 40 quarters is 10 years. Less than 10 years might be required, however, because the hours that your spouse or parents (if you are a minor) work may count.

LAWFUL PERMANENT RESIDENTS

This means that, aside from the above-mentioned exceptions, most LPRs will have to wait at least 10 years before becoming eligible to apply for SSI. However, if you naturalize after five years of being an LPR, you will not have to wait, because you will become eligible to apply for SSI as a U.S. citizen.

How Do I Apply for SSI?
To see if you qualify for SSI and to set up an appointment to apply, contact the Social Security Administration at 1-800-772-1213 or go online to www.ssa.gov. You can find your local Social Security office online at www.socialsecurity.gov/locator. You may need the following documents:

- Social Security number (if you do not have one, you may receive one if the Social Security Administration decides you are eligible for SSI)
- Proof of age (see the Guide's Chapter 7, "Case Status and Proof of Status," for documents you can use)
- Proof of citizenship (see Chapter 7 for documents you can use)
- Proof of income (paychecks if you work)
- Proof of resources (bank statements, deeds or tax statements if you own property, life or disability insurance policies, titles or registrations for vehicles)
- Proof of living arrangements (lease or rent receipt for your apartment, deed or property tax bill, receipts or information on household expenses such as utilities)

Does My State Have a Similar Program for Which I May Be Eligible?
Some states have programs similar to SSI for which you may be eligible even if you are not eligible for SSI. For a list of these programs, see NILC's *Guide to Immigrant Eligibility for Federal Programs* at http://nilc.org/guideupdate.html, and click on Table 9: State-Funded SSI Replacement Programs.

LAWFUL PERMANENT RESIDENTS

Can I Apply for the Food Stamp Program (SNAP)?
SNAP, or food stamps, provides vouchers or coupons to low-income people (people who do not make a lot of money) that can be used to buy food.

As an LPR, you must have been in status for five years, OR have 40 qualifying quarters of work, to receive food stamps. However, you may not have to wait five years if you meet any of the following criteria:

- Under 18 years old, or
- Disabled or blind and receiving benefits or assistance for this, or
- Were born before August 22, 1931 and were lawfully residing in the U.S. on August 22, 1996, or
- A member of a Hmong or Laotian tribe that aided the U.S. military in Vietnam, or
- American Indian.

In a crisis, you can get emergency food stamps quickly. This is called "expedited food stamps." An example of a crisis is being homeless and without food or low income with many children.

How Do I Apply for SNAP?
Each state has its own application, so you will need to contact your local Food Stamp office or social service office to request one. To find your local Food Stamp office call 1-800-221-5689 or go online to www.fns.usda.gov/snap/.

Can I Apply for Temporary Assistance for Needy Families (TANF)?
TANF provides cash assistance for low-income families with children who are in the U.S.

LAWFUL PERMANENT RESIDENTS

If you are an LPR, you must have been in status for five years before being eligible for TANF benefits. However, qualified immigrant veterans, active duty military members, and military spouses or children are immediately eligible, provided they meet the other program requirements.

Since a child born in the U.S. is automatically a U.S. citizen, immigrant parents of a U.S. citizen child can also apply to get TANF for their child, even if they themselves are not eligible.

Important! TANF is the federal term for the program, but because it is state-run, it will likely have a different name in your state. Check with the state eligibility worker at the state agency or your refugee case worker for the correct name. It is very important that you check with your state, even if you do not think you are eligible, because your state's rules may be different and you may actually be eligible. Check NILC's guide for your state's program and eligibility at http://nilc.org/guide_tanf.html.

How Do I Apply for TANF?
Contact your local state social services office to learn more. You can also find out more about the TANF program if you call 202-401-5139 or go online to www.acf.hhs.gov/programs/ofa/.

How Long May I Receive TANF?
You may receive for up to five years after you become eligible, or until your income exceeds the income ceiling. It will also be terminated before the time limit expires if your children are no longer minors, or if you do not respond to requests to supply updated information on your income and assets.

LAWFUL PERMANENT RESIDENTS

Are There Requirements I Must Meet to Continue to Receive TANF?
TANF has a work participation activity requirement. This program has different rules in each state or local area. Be sure to find out the rule in your state and what you must do or your benefits will be stopped due to "non-compliance" (not following the rules).

If you believe your benefits were stopped in error, you have the right to appeal. The appeal process must be explained to you in a language you understand.

Can I Apply for CHIP (Children's Health Insurance Program)?
CHIP provides free or low-cost health coverage to children up to age 19. Some states provide more coverage than others, but CHIP is available in every state.

If you are an LPR, you must have been in status for five years before becoming eligible for CHIP benefits. However, qualified immigrant veterans, active duty military members, and military spouses or children are immediately eligible, provided they meet the other program requirements. Additionally, it is very important that you check with your state, even if you do not think you are eligible, because the rules may be different in your state.

Important! Since a child born in the U.S. is automatically a U.S. citizen, immigrant parents of a U.S. citizen child can also apply to get CHIP for their child, even if they themselves are not eligible.

To learn more about CHIP, you can call 1-877-KIDS-NOW (1-877-543-7669), or visit http://insurekidsnow.gov/state/index.html and click on your state. Each state may have slightly different requirements.

LAWFUL PERMANENT RESIDENTS

Additional Programs for Families
You are always eligible for the following services, regardless of status.

Women, Infants and Children (WIC)
WIC is a national program that provides food vouchers or coupons, health care referrals, and nutrition education for low-income pregnant women, mothers up to a year after having a child, and children under five years old. Call 1-800-WIC-WINS (1-800-942-9467) or go online to www.fns.usda.gov/wic/ to find the office nearest you.

Early Head Start and Head Start
Early Head Start and Head Start are child care programs that focus on education, health, and social development. For more information, contact your local school or the Head Start Bureau online at www.acf.hhs.gov/programs/ohs or 1-202-205-8572.

Meal Programs
Free breakfast and lunch programs are offered by some schools for their students. These programs may serve children all year long. Contact your local public school for more information or ask about this when you enroll your children in school.

Healthcare
Emergency Medicaid covers childbirth regardless of immigrations status, as long as the mother meets the low-income requirements.

Additional Programs
Your state may offer additional programs. Contact your local social services office.

LAWFUL PERMANENT RESIDENTS

Do I Have Access to Healthcare?

Lawful permanent residents have access to some forms of healthcare, but not as many as U.S. citizens. You have access to emergency medical care, may have limited access to Medicare and Medicaid (dependent on various factors), and are eligible for new options under the Affordable Care Act. These healthcare options as they apply to LPRs are explained briefly below. For further details, please see Chapter 19, "How to Access Healthcare," in the Guide.

Emergency Medical Care
Everyone, regardless of immigration status, may be eligible to receive

- Federally-funded state medical assistance for emergency care, which includes emergency Medicaid, emergency room care, and labor and delivery
- Short-term, non-cash, in-kind disaster relief
- Public health assistance for immunizations and testing and treatment for communicable diseases
- Assistance that provides in-kind services to the community (donations), does not make the donation dependent on your income or resources, and is necessary for your protection or safety (such as soup kitchens, short-term shelters, and crisis counseling or intervention)

If you ever experience a life-threatening emergency, including physical danger, crime, fire, or medical emergencies, dial 911 from any phone for access to emergency services.

Can I Access Refugee Medical Assistance (RMA)?
No, as an LPR, you are not eligible for Refugee Medical Assistance (RMA).

LAWFUL PERMANENT RESIDENTS

Can I Access Medicaid?
Medicaid is a program that helps pay for your healthcare costs if you are low-income (if you do not make a lot of money) and are of working age. If you are an LPR, you must have been in status for five years before becoming eligible for Medicaid benefits. However, if you are an LPR under 21 years of age, or a pregnant woman of any age, you may be eligible to receive Medicaid benefits immediately.

Note: About half the states use their own money to provide Medicaid to children and/or pregnant women who are either qualified immigrants or lawfully residing in the U.S. (both of which apply to LPRs) without a waiting period. A few states provide medical assistance to additional groups of immigrants who are ineligible for federal Medicaid, using their own funds. Therefore, it is very important that you check with your state, even if you do not think you are eligible, because the rules may be different in your state.

How Long Can I Use Medicaid?
You may be eligible to use Medicaid for up to seven years after you arrive or are approved under your qualifying status, or until your income exceeds the income ceiling. However, keep in mind that if you naturalize (become a U.S. citizen) these immigration-related time limits will no longer apply to you.

How Do I Apply for Medicaid?
Go to your local social services office to apply for Medicaid. The name for this office is different in each state.

Can I Access Medicare?
Medicare is a health insurance program for people who are age 65 or older or who have certain disabilities. If you meet either of these

LAWFUL PERMANENT RESIDENTS

criteria, you may qualify for Part A "Premium Free," which covers the cost of inpatient care while you are in the hospital. Medicare Part A is available to some statuses, but the rules are very complex, and depend on how much U.S. work experience you have, among other criteria. Ask your state social services provider or case manager for help.

Part B "Buy in" Medicare, which covers doctors' services and outpatient hospital care, has similar criteria. LPRs are eligible for Part B after having LPR status for five years.

If you are low-income, your state may help you pay for Part A and/or Part B Medicare. For more information, go online to www.socialsecurity.gov or call Social Security at 1-800-772-1213. You can also make an appointment with your local Social Security office. Go online to www.socialsecurity.gov/locator. For more information on Medicare, go online to www.medicare.gov.

Am I Eligible for New Options for Health Insurance from the Patient Protection and Affordable Care Act (ACA)?

The Affordable Care Act (ACA), also known as "Obamacare," improves access to healthcare for many immigrants. Among other things, the ACA created new health insurance "Marketplaces" or "exchanges." These exchanges provide a new way for you to find health insurance that fits your health and budgetary needs. The plans on the exchanges are owned by private insurance companies, and you can compare the plans side by side. No one can turn you down for illnesses or medical conditions you already have.

As an LPR, you are eligible for the new options under the Marketplace. You are also eligible to apply for premium tax credits to pay for plans purchased under the exchanges. Some non-pregnant adults,

LAWFUL PERMANENT RESIDENTS

including some immigrants, will become eligible for their state's Medicaid program.

How to Apply
You will need to fill out a single application for the Marketplace, and there are many resources available to help you. You can access the Marketplace at www.healthcare.gov, or by calling 1-800-318-2596. You may also send a paper application in the mail to:

Health Insurance Marketplace
Department of Health and Human Services
465 Industrial Blvd.
London, KY 40750

The application for Marketplace insurance now appears in over 30 languages at http://marketplace.cms.gov/applications-and-forms/individuals-and-families-forms.html.

Your state may run its own Marketplace, or it may use the Federal Marketplace. You can learn about your state's system and where to apply in your state at www.healthcare.gov/what-is-the-marketplace-in-my-state.

It is recommended that you get someone to help you review the plans available to you, decide which plan fits your particular needs best, and apply. You can find help from a Marketplace "Navigator," or someone whose job it is to help you understand the Marketplace, by going online to https://localhelp.healthcare.gov and filling in where you live.

In order to learn more about the Affordable Care Act, how to sign up, and what it means for you and your family, please see www.healthcare.gov/immigration-status-and-the-marketplace/.

LAWFUL PERMANENT RESIDENTS

Additional Tips
A "Healthy Living Toolkit," which covers information about healthcare, hygiene, and physical and mental health, can be found at www.refugees.org/resources/for-refugees--immigrants/health/. Additionally, ORR (Office of Refugee Resettlement) has helpful resources on healthcare for immigrants at www.acf.hhs.gov/programs/orr/health.

Federally qualified health centers provide medical care to individuals regardless of immigration status, and often work on a sliding scale. That means you pay only what you are able based on your income. Go to www.bphc.hrsa.gov and type your zip code in the "find a Health Center" box to locate a health center near you.

Dental care is care for your teeth. It is important to make regular dental check-ups twice a year and call the dentist if you have tooth pain, because problems with your teeth can cause many other dangerous health problems, including heart disease. Often schools where students are studying to be dentists will offer affordable or even free dental work. Look in the phone book or online for listings of area universities and colleges that have dental schools or free/low cost dental clinics.

If you were in immigration detention and saw a doctor while detained, it is important that you get your medical records from detention. See Chapter 6, "How to Get Your Personal Property After You Are Released from Detention," in the Guide.

Important! Emotional and mental health are considered just as important as physical health in the U.S. If you feel depressed, anxious, scared, or overwhelmed, it is important that you seek help from a therapist, social worker, or other mental health service provider. The Substance Abuse and Mental Health Services

LAWFUL PERMANENT RESIDENTS

Administration (SAMHSA) provides information about service providers throughout the country. You can use SAMHSA's online service provider locator at http://store.samhsa.gov/mhlocator or you can call 1-877-726-4727 (1-877-SAMHSA7).

Sometimes people become so depressed, they consider committing suicide. If you or someone you know feels suicidal, call the National Suicide Prevention Hotline immediately at 1-800-SUICIDE (1-800-784-2433) or 1-888-SUICIDE (1-888-784-2433). For Spanish, dial 1-877-SUICIDA (1-877-784-2432).

See Chapter 23, "How to Get Emotional Support," in the Guide for more details.

Do I Have Access to Affordable Housing?

LPRs are eligible for many public housing programs in the U.S. To learn more about housing programs in the U.S., please see Chapter 20, "How to Access Housing," in the Guide. Some additional resources are listed below:

If you are homeless and need shelter, see www.homelessshelterdirectory.org/ for a list of homeless shelters in your state.

If you or your children are the victim of abuse by your partner or spouse and you are afraid to stay in your home, call the National Domestic Violence Hotline at 1-800-799-7233 or 1-800-787-3224 or go online to www.thehotline.org.

If you are low-income, elderly, or have a disability, you may be eligible for public housing. To participate, you must fit the eligibility criteria, pay a portion of rent dependent on your income, and live

LAWFUL PERMANENT RESIDENTS

in a public housing project. For more information, please visit http://portal.hud.gov/hudportal/HUD?src=/topics/rental_assistance/phprog. You may also be eligible for subsidized housing through the Housing Choice Vouchers Program, which provides more choice in housing, but requires you to find housing where the landlord agrees to participate. For more information, please visit http://portal.hud.gov/hudportal/HUD?src=/program_offices/public_indian_housing/programs/hcv/about.

Can I Access Childcare and Education?

As an LPR, there are many valuable opportunities in the U.S. for you and your children to pursue an education. A few important status-specific points are below, but please see Chapter 21, "How to Access Childcare and Education," in the Guide for more information.

Important! In the U.S., leaving your children at home alone is often considered "neglect," a form of child abuse. If you leave your child at home alone, the state government may take your child away from you. Check with your state's child welfare agency to learn the age requirements in your state: www.childwelfare.gov/pubs/reslist/rl_dsp_website.cfm?rs_ID=16&rate_chno=AZ-0004E.

Head Start: Childcare for Children Under Five
In case family or friends are not available to care for your children while you work, Head Start is a federal program that cares for young children and prepares them for school. Eligibility is based on financial need. To learn more, see http://eclkc.ohs.acf.hhs.gov/hslc/hs/about.

Primary and Secondary Education for Children Ages 5-18
In the U.S., every child, regardless of their immigration status, has the right to a free public education kindergarten through grade

LAWFUL PERMANENT RESIDENTS

12. If you are the parent or guardian of a child under the age of 18, by law you are required to send them to school. Some states require school attendance only through age 16. Visit your state's Board of Education website for more information.

Education Options for Adults
If you are 16 or older and have not completed high school, you can enroll in Adult Secondary Education (ASE) classes. These classes prepare you to earn a GED (General Education Development) certificate. A GED certificate is an alternative to a high school diploma. For more information about the exam, or to locate a testing center, please visit www.gedtestingservice.com/ged-testing-service.

For information on higher educational opportunities such as college or university, as well as the enrollment process, please visit www.collegeboard.org/.

As an LPR, you are eligible for student financial aid from the U.S. Department of Education. Financial aid includes work study programs, the Pell grant, and certain government loans such as the Stafford and Perkins loans. To learn more visit www.studentaid.ed.gov or www.fafsa.ed.gov. You may also visit the U.S. Department of Education at www.ed.gov or call 1-800-USA-LEARN (1-800-872-5327), and call the Federal Student Aid Information Center at 1-800-433-3243.

If you have any questions, concerns, or comments about this supplement, or the *First Steps* guide, please contact the Detained Torture Survivors' Legal Support Network at Lutheran Immigration and Refugee Service at firststeps@lirs.org.

ACKNOWLEDGMENTS

This supplement to *First Steps* has been brought to you by the Detained Torture Survivors' Legal Support Network, a program of LIRS's Access to Justice Unit. This supplement was co-authored by Angela Edman, Staff Attorney for LIRS's Access to Justice (ATJ) program, and Sarah Vail, LIRS Programs and Protection Administrative Assistant.

LIRS encourages printing and distribution of this supplement. Information in this manual may be reprinted with the following note: Reprinted with permission of the Detained Torture Survivors' Legal Support Network, a program of Lutheran Immigration and Refugee Service.

Printed in 2014

CPSIA information can be obtained at www.ICGtesting.com
Printed in the USA
BVOW03s1758081014

369942BV00004B/8/P